— CONTINENTS —

EUROPE

Galadriel Watson

WEIGL PUBLISHERS INC.

Published by Weigl Publishers Inc.
350 5ᵗʰ Avenue, Suite 3304, PMB 6G
New York, NY 10118-0069 USA
Web site: www.weigl.com

Library of Congress Cataloging-in-Publication Data

Watson, Galadriel Findlay.
  Europe / Galadriel Watson.
      p. cm. -- (Continents)
  Includes bibliographical references and index.
  ISBN 1-59036-320-5 (hard cover : alk. paper) -- ISBN 1-59036-327-2
(soft cover : alk. paper)
  1. Europe--Juvenile literature. I. Title. II. Continents (New York, N.Y.)
  D1051.W27 2005
  940--dc22
                                                    2005004388

Printed in the United States of America
1 2 3 4 5 6 7 8 9 10 09 08 07 06 05

All of the Internet URLs given in the book were valid at the time of publication. However, due to the dynamic nature of the Internet, some addresses may have changed, or sites may have ceased to exist since publication. While the author and publisher regret any inconvenience this may cause readers, no responsibility for any such changes can be accepted by either the author or the publisher.

Project Coordinator
Heather C. Hudak

Substantive Editor
Heather Kissock

Layout
Kathryn Livingstone
Gregg Muller

Designer
Terry Paulhus

Photo Researcher
Kim Winiski

— CONTINENTS —
EUROPE

TABLE OF CONTENTS

Introduction

Although Europe's area is small, it is a land filled with **diversity**. Its warm coastal waters attract millions of sunbathers each year, while skiers and climbers adore the continent's high mountain peaks. Europe has modern cities and open fields of wheat and oats, as well as glittering glass skyscrapers and crumbling **medieval** castles.

Of the world's seven continents, only Australia is smaller than Europe in size. Europe covers an area of over 4 million square miles (10.4 million square kilometers), or about 7 percent of Earth's land. Just because it is small in size, however, does not mean Europe has a small population. In fact, only the continents of Asia and Africa have more people than Europe.

The Castel Sant'Angelo in Rome was built between AD 135 and 139. Popes used it as a place of refuge during the Middle Ages. Today, a tunnel connects it to the Vatican.

European peoples have played very important roles throughout world history. Their influence on arts, science, politics, philosophy, and religion dates as far back as 3000 BC. European efforts to explore new lands and expand trade markets led to the creation of many countries, from Canada and the United States to Australia and South Africa.

Today, Europe consists of 47 countries. Many are well known, such as Great Britain, France, and Italy. Georgia, Moldova, and Malta are lesser known outside European borders.

Russia is Europe's largest country. At about twice the size of the United States, it is also the largest country in the world. Russia is located partly in Europe, partly in Asia. Many of its citizens live on the European side of the country. Russia's capital city, Moscow, is Europe's largest city.

Vatican City is Europe's—and the world's—smallest country. Surrounded by the Italian city of Rome, Vatican City covers only 0.17 square miles (0.44 sq km). Vatican City is the headquarters of the Roman Catholic Church and home to the pope.

Europe

Europe is located in the Northern Hemisphere. Its northern boundary is the Arctic Ocean. It is bordered on the west by the Atlantic Ocean. The Mediterranean Sea, the Black Sea, and the Caucasus Mountains border Europe to the south.

Europe's eastern boundary is difficult to determine. On its east side, Europe is attached to the continent of Asia. Some geographers believe Europe and Asia should not be considered two separate continents. They believe Europe and Asia are part of a larger continent called Eurasia. Other geographers believe Europe is a distinct continent. Many of these geographers agree the boundary between Europe and Asia includes the Ural Mountains, the Ural River, and the Caspian Sea. The European continent also includes many islands, such as Great Britain, Ireland, and Iceland.

At one time, Eurasian brown bears were taught to dance at carnivals and festivals. Today, they are often found in zoos.

European Continent Map

GREENLAND

ICELAND

SWEDEN

FINLAND

NORWAY

ESTONIA

LATVIA

DENMARK

LITHUANIA

RUSSIA

IRELAND

U. K.

BELARUS

NETH.

GERMANY

ATLANTIC
OCEAN

BELGIUM

POLAND

LUX.

UKRAINE

CZECH

SLOVAKIA

MOLDOVA

LIECH.

AUSTRIA

HUNGARY

SWITZERLAND

SLOVENIA

ROMANIA

GEORGIA

FRANCE

CROATIA

BOSNIA
and
HERZ.

ANDORRA

YUGOSLAVIA

BULGARIA

PORTUGAL

SPAIN

MACEDONIA

TURKEY

ITALY

ALBANIA

GREECE

SYRIA

IRAQ

MOROCCO

JORDAN

N

ALGERIA

TUNISIA

SAUDI ARABIA

W   E

| 0 | 125 | 250 | 375 | 500 | MILES |
| 0 | 201 | 402 | 604 | 805 | KILOMETERS |

S

LIBYA

The Little Mermaid statue is a well-known
symbol of Copenhagen, Denmark. The statue
has attracted nearly one million visitors each
year since she was sculpted in 1913.

Location and Resources

Land and Climate

*E*urope can be divided into four geographic regions: the Northwest Mountains, the Great European Plain, the Central Uplands, and the Alpine Mountains. In the Northwest Mountains, the mountains are so old that most have eroded. The Great European Plain in the south and in Russia offers some of the world's best farmland and is home to many of Europe's residents. The Central Uplands consist of low mountains and large **plateaus**. Finally, several mountain chains cross southern Europe. These include the Alps, the Pyrenees, and the Caucasus Mountains. Most of these areas are suitable for human habitation. Only a few places, such as in the extreme north or on mountaintops, are unable to support life.

The Dolomite mountain range in northern Italy forms part of the Alps. Eighteen of the Alps's impressive peaks are more than 10,000 feet (3,050 meters) high.

Much of the European continent has mild weather. Winds blow across the Atlantic Ocean, where the Gulf Stream current warms them. These warm winds sweep across the continent, keeping the land at moderate temperatures. Most European countries have four seasons. In these countries, winter occurs between November and March. Summer takes place between June and September.

In general, areas in northern and eastern Europe have longer, colder winters and shorter, cooler summers than places in the south or west. Northern Europe has the coldest climates on the continent. In some northern regions, during the bitter winter months, there is little or no daylight. The Sun shines 24 hours per day in the summer. Central Europe has overcast, rainy winters with moderate summers. In southern Europe, the summers are hot, and the winters are mild with little rain.

Fast Facts

Europe's highest mountain is Mount El'brus in Russia. It rises 18,510 feet (5,642 m) above sea level.

Europe's longest river is the Volga River. It flows 2,194 miles (3,531 km) from Russia to the Caspian Sea.

Europe and the other continents once belonged to a huge landmass called Pangaea. Over time, this giant continent broke apart. Europe took its current shape about 5 million years ago.

Salzburg, Austria, is located near the Alps. The city has cold, dry winters and warm summers.

Plants and Animals

*E*urope's plant life is found in three zones: forests, grasslands, and tundra. Although most European forests have been cut down, large areas exist in northern countries. Smaller patches of forest are located further south. Trees, such as the cork tree and the olive tree, grow along the Mediterranean coast.

Grasslands—from the prairies to the **steppes**—are covered with various grasses. Tundra areas and mountain peaks are cold and treeless. Plant life in these regions includes small shrubs, wildflowers, and lichens.

Most European animals thrive only in wildlife reserves or in places that are difficult for people to access. Other animals live in zoos. Europe has many small animals, such as rabbits, squirrels, badgers, hedgehogs, moles, and lemmings.

Reindeer live in Europe's cold tundra regions. Other tundra animals include the Arctic fox and snowy owl.

Animals in Europe's forests include wolves, elks, and European brown bears. Wild boars and lizards live around the Mediterranean Sea. Rodents, such as marmots and field mice, live in the continent's grassland areas, as do many kinds of birds and insects. Seals and fish, such as anchovy, cod, salmon, and tuna, live in Europe's coastal waters.

Fast Facts

The dwarf birch and lady's-slipper orchid are some of Europe's **endangered** plant species.

At one time, forests covered about 80 percent of Europe. They now cover only about 30 percent of the land. People began cutting down forests in the 800s and have continued to do so throughout history.

Prehistoric cave drawings throughout Europe show extinct animals such as mammoths and **aurochs**. At one time, Europe was also home to elephants and wild horses.

Endangered animal species in Europe include the golden eagle, loggerhead turtle, horseshoe bat, and swallowtail butterfly.

Europe's largest mammal is the European bison. About 3,000 European bison still exist, many in Poland's Bialowieza National Park.

Every 30 to 35 years, huge numbers of Norway lemmings swarm through northern **Scandinavia**.

Natural Resources

Europeans are blessed with many natural advantages. For example, Europe has some of the world's best farmland. In fact, more than half of the continent is covered with farms. About half of Europe's cropland is used to grow grains such as barley, oats, and wheat. More than 90 percent of the world's rye comes from Europe. Other farmers raise livestock, such as sheep, cattle, and pigs, producing more than 30 percent of the world's meat.

Fishing is important to Europe's coastal countries. European countries—particularly Norway and Russia—catch about 25 percent of all the fish caught in the world.

Europe is rich in minerals. It has a large supply of coal, which is used mainly to provide power to industries. Europe also has a large amount of uranium, which is used in **nuclear reactors**. Other important minerals found in Europe include lead, nickel, platinum, and zinc.

Some northern countries, such as Sweden and Finland, specialize in producing timber.

Fast Facts

Lead is no longer used to make pencils. Instead, the mineral graphite, found in England, Austria, and the Czech Republic, is mixed with clay to make the lead-like substance now used to make pencils.

Many European crops are not native to the continent. They originally came with settlers from other continents. Wheat, for example, came from Ethiopia in Africa. Oats came from China in Asia. Potatoes came from South America.

In the United Kingdom, only about 1 percent of employed individuals work in agriculture. In Albania, about 50 percent of employed people work in this industry.

Great Britain is home to more sheep than any other European country. In 2003, there were more than 35.7 million sheep on British farms.

Economy

Tourism

The tourism industry is very important to many European countries. This industry employs a large number of Europeans and brings money to local economies. Of all the money spent on tourism worldwide in 1 year, 60 percent is spent traveling to and within Europe.

Each year, for example, more than 50 million people visit Italy. Two million tourists also travel to tiny San Marino—a 23-square mile (60-sq km) republic in southern Europe. Switzerland is also quite small—only 15,942 square miles (41,290 sq km)—yet it attracts nearly 12 million visitors each year.

Originally built around AD 70, the Roman Colosseum seated about 50,000 people. Today, it is the best-known ancient building in Rome. The Colosseum attracts more than 4 million tourists each year.

The continent's natural beauty is one of its major draws. Visitors soak in the Sun along the beaches of the Riviera, on Greek islands, or at resorts along the Black Sea. Skiers head to the Alps or to one of Europe's many other mountain ranges. Other visitors enjoy the beauty of England's Lake District or Norway's whale-watching boat rides.

Those in search of beautiful architecture often journey to Europe. **Gothic** cathedrals reach skyward in places such as France and Germany. Castles—some crumbling and some still in use—are found across the continent. The Kremlin, in Moscow, Russia, was once a fortress. Its buildings are now home to several museums.

Venice, Italy, attracts many visitors with its **canals** and historic buildings. Other tourists visit the Netherlands to see fields of colorful tulips and windmills, or France to sit and watch the world go by from one of its sidewalk cafés. With numerous churches and towers, Prague, the capital of the Czech Republic, is considered by many to be one of Eastern Europe's most beautiful cities. Another old and picturesque city is Koblenz in Germany. Situated on the Rhine River, its historic downtown was destroyed in World War II. It has since been restored and is a popular tourist destination.

Fast Facts

The Louvre Museum in Paris, France, is one of Europe's oldest museums. It dates back to 1793 and houses many collections, including Islamic art and Egyptian antiquities.

Pompeii is an ancient Roman town that was buried in ash after Mount Vesuvius, a nearby volcano, erupted in AD 79.

Many visitors marvel at Northern Ireland's Giant's Causeway. It is an **outcropping** of volcanic rocks cooled into strange, six-sided columns.

The London Eye, a unique British attraction, is the world's biggest observation wheel.

The wrought-iron Eiffel Tower, built for the 1889 World's Fair, attracts many people to Paris, France.

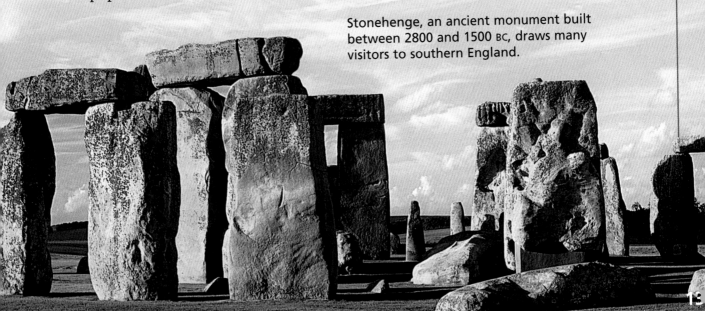

Stonehenge, an ancient monument built between 2800 and 1500 BC, draws many visitors to southern England.

Industry

*I*n addition to Europe's abundant natural resources, European industry benefits from another resource—a highly skilled work force. Together, these strengths have made Europe one of the world's leading industrial centers. Industry in western Europe is more developed than in eastern Europe. Many countries in western Europe use the latest technologies to produce huge quantities of goods. Other countries, especially those in Eastern Europe, use older methods and produce fewer goods. In total, only the United States manufactures more items than Europe.

Europe's industrial strength is not surprising considering that industry originated in Europe. The **Industrial Revolution** began in 1730 in northern England, when the water-driven machine was invented. The machine's first purpose was to spin and weave wool and cotton, but it was soon adapted to other activities. The main benefit of using machines was that more products could be made in less time and for less cost.

There have been farms on Salisbury Plain in southern England for thousands of years.

Goods and Services

European manufactured goods are found all over the world. Volkswagen and Volvo vehicles, for example, originated in Europe. Swiss watches and chocolate, Parisian fashions, and English toffee are also well-known worldwide. Romania is one of the world's top ten producers of wine. European manufacturers also produce goods such as medical drugs, synthetic rubber, steel, and fertilizers.

Services are also important to the European economy. Some of the world's largest banks are based in Great Britain, France, Germany, and Switzerland. Major **stock exchanges** are located in Amsterdam, Frankfurt, London, Paris, and Zurich. Europe is home to some of the world's largest **merchant shipping fleets**. Many of the world's largest armies are also found in Europe. Other Europeans work in education, health care, and research.

Fast Facts

After Japan and the United States, Germany manufactures the most cars in the world.

The wealth of European countries varies widely. Oil-rich Norway, for example, produces US $42,222 of goods and services per person each year. This is the highest of any country in the world. Moldova, on the other hand, produces only $398.

In most European nations, more than 90 percent of the people can read and write. This makes Europeans among the best-educated people in the world.

Volkswagen employs thousands of Europeans in car-building factories.

The Past

Indigenous Peoples

People have lived in Europe for thousands of years. Archaeologists have found fossils and tools showing humans lived on the continent more than 700,000 years ago. One species, called the Neanderthals, lived between 130,000 and 35,000 years ago. These people are now extinct. Ancestors of modern humans first appeared about 40,000 years ago.

In ancient times, humans in Europe lived in various tribes. These were small groups that searched the land for food. By about 6000 BC, people living in southeastern Europe discovered they could grow food by farming and no longer needed to live as **nomads**. The villages of these people became Europe's first settlements. The idea of farming spread to most of the rest of Europe by about 3000 BC. Later, civilizations began to grow around the Mediterranean Sea. The best-known of these civilizations are those of Ancient Greece and Rome.

Fast Facts

Early tribes in Great Britain included the Angles, Celts, Danes, Jutes, and Saxons.

Ancient Greece was strongest between 400 and 300 BC. The **Roman Empire** was at its peak from 27 BC to AD 180, when it encompassed much of Europe, as well as parts of Asia and Africa.

The continent we now call Europe was named Europa by the Ancient Greeks. It probably meant "mainland."

Beginning in 776 BC, the Olympic games were held every 4 years in Olympia, Greece. Today, the Olympics are held all over the world.

The Age of Exploration

From the early 1300s to the late 1500s, Europe experienced the Renaissance. This was a period when Europeans were very interested in the arts and sciences, a time when many great ideas and works were produced.

One of the results of the Renaissance was the desire to explore. In the 1400s, Spanish and Portuguese explorers traveled farther than any Europeans had in the past. Explorers ventured to lands of which Europeans had no previous knowledge. Vasco da Gama captained the first voyage from Europe to India, via Africa. Christopher Columbus reached the Caribbean. Ferdinand Magellan became the first European to sail around the world. Soon, explorers from many other European countries were making new discoveries. In 1497, John Cabot, on behalf of Great Britain, was the first European to land in North America since the Vikings had traveled there in 985 BC.

Portuguese explorer Vasco da Gama helped establish trade routes and create the Portuguese Empire.

Fast Facts

After the decline of the Roman Empire, the Roman Catholic Church held most of the power throughout Europe. This period is known as the Middle Ages.

Many European explorers sailed the world in hopes of finding a faster **trade** route to Asia. In Asia, ships could be loaded with valuable items such as spices and silks.

Vikings were from Scandinavia. Some Vikings sailed from Europe to other continents.

Italian-born explorer John Cabot landed in North America while searching for a western route to Asia. He gained King Henry the VII's permission to sail for Great Britain.

Early Settlers

*I*n many of the areas where Europeans explored, they started settlements called **colonies**. They built colonies in North America, Africa, and South America. European countries wanted colonies for many reasons. First, they could access natural resources, such as cotton, that European industries could manufacture into goods. European countries sold these manufactured goods back to the colonies and earned profits. Colonists could also find and send valuable items such as beaver furs and gold to Europe for European use.

Europeans moved to the colonies for many reasons, too. Some missionaries wanted to convert indigenous peoples to European religions. Others belonged to religious groups, such as Huguenots, Quakers, Jews, and Moravians, that wanted to escape **persecution** in Europe. Others wanted free or inexpensive land, employment, and the hope of a better future.

Over time, a large portion of the world came under the control of European nations. By the mid-1700s, India was under British control. Portugal established Brazil. Eventually, almost all of Africa and about one-third of Asia were colonized. In the 1500s, the English, French, Spanish, Dutch, and Swedish began colonizing North America.

European governments built trading posts to buy and sell goods in many North American colonies. Many cities and towns grew around the sites of these early trading posts, including Grand Portage, Minnesota.

Colonies forced many indigenous peoples to change their ways of life. Men, women, and children were captured in West Africa and sent to other colonies as **slaves**. Many Native-American peoples died from European diseases. Some civilizations, such as the Incas in South America, were completely destroyed by European settlers.

Today, people still **emigrate** from Europe to other countries around the world. Since the early 1800s, about 60 million people have left Europe. More than half of these people moved to the United States. People from other countries also move to Europe. Many are attracted by Europe's need for workers. These people take jobs in areas such as the construction industry and health care.

Europeans built plantations to grow crops in North American colonies.

Culture

Population

About 700 million people live in Europe. In 1900, Europe was home to about one-quarter of all the world's population. Today, only about one-eighth of Earth's population lives on the continent. About 105 million people live in Russia's European portion, making it Europe's most populated country. With a population of about 1,000, Vatican City has the fewest citizens of any European country.

In general, areas such as northern Europe, as well as mountainous locations, have the lowest populations. Many people live in an area that stretches from England through northern France and Germany to Moscow in Russia. Many more live in an area extending from Germany south to Italy. Monaco has the highest population **density**—about 42,500 people live on each square mile (2.6 sq km) of land. Iceland has the lowest population density, with about 7 people per square mile (2.7 per sq km). On average, Europe has about 78 people per square mile (30 per sq km).

The Hungarian capital of Budapest is home to about 2 million people.

Politics and Government

In Europe, kings or queens rule some countries. These countries are called monarchies. In some monarchies, citizens also elect officials to represent them in the government. These are called constitutional monarchies. In democracies or republics, all the officials are elected.

Communist countries are those in which the government owns most of the country's property and wealth. The government controls money and goods so that they are equally shared by the people. After World War II, many communist countries were established in Eastern Europe. The former Soviet Union and the former East Germany are two examples of communist countries. By the late 1980s, many people in these countries wanted more freedom. A large number of communist governments fell from power.

Today, many European countries have joined the European Union. The countries have agreed to work together in areas such as trade, immigration, and military policy. They have also decided to use a common currency called the euro.

Fast Facts

Monaco is a monarchy. The Grimaldi family has ruled the country since 1308.

Portugal was a **dictatorship** from 1933 to 1968. Its citizens could not decide who would lead their country, and they could not choose another leader.

When the Soviet Union's communist government fell in 1991, the country divided into 15 separate countries. The largest country is Russia.

King Ludwig II of Bavaria built Neuschwanstein Castle in Germany. This castle inspired the Sleeping Beauty Castle in Disneyland, California.

Cultural Groups

Europe is home to more than 150 cultural groups. In ancient times, vast stretches of mountains, forests, or marshlands separated European tribes. Few people traveled between tribes. As a result, each group developed its own way of life. Cultural groups today, therefore, have differing backgrounds and traditions based on these ancient ways of life. Some cultures also have distinct languages, **dialects**, or religions.

Europe is home to about 50 languages and more than 100 dialects. In general, European languages can be divided into three groups. Germanic languages came from the tribal language of southern Scandinavia. They include German, Swedish, and Icelandic. Romance languages include French, Spanish, and Italian. They came from the Roman Empire's Latin language. Slavic languages formed in Europe's eastern and southeastern areas, as well as Russia. They include Polish, Russian, and Bulgarian. Languages such as Greek, Baltic, and Romany are unlike other European languages.

Ancient Greeks built many structures that exist today. The Acropolis in Athens, Greece, was built about 2,500 years ago.

Most Europeans are **Christian**. Many, particularly those in western and southwestern Europe, belong to the Roman Catholic Church. Those in the east and southeast are generally Eastern Orthodox, while those in the north are generally Protestant. Other Europeans may be Jewish or Muslim.

Despite their different backgrounds, many Europeans consider themselves to belong to the country in which they live. Others think of themselves only as European. They take pride in the continent's exceptional history and its outstanding artistic, scientific, and political achievements.

St. Mary's Church is one of the most important places of worship in Krakow, Poland.

Arts and Entertainment

Europeans have produced art since ancient times. The Greeks and Romans built monuments that still stand today. They sculpted works of art, wrote books, and staged plays.

In the **visual arts**, many artistic movements originated in Europe and have influenced artists around the world. Spain's Pablo Picasso used **cubism** to show many points of view of an object or person, all at the same time. Another Spaniard, Salvador Dalí, produced unique paintings as part of the **surrealist** movement.

Many European musicians are also well known around the world. The world's first opera was performed in Europe in the 1590s. The world's first symphony was composed in Europe in the 1700s. Well-known composers include Johann Sebastian Bach, Ludwig van Beethoven, and Amadeus Mozart. More recent pop musicians include The Beatles, The Rolling Stones, U2, ABBA, and The Cardigans.

One of Russia's major art forms is ballet. Its ballet companies include the world-famous Kirov Ballet of St. Petersburg and Moscow's Bolshoi Theatre Ballet. Spaniards enjoy **flamenco dancing**, as well other traditional pastimes, including singing folk songs.

Michelangelo Buonarotti was an Italian artist who painted the ceiling of the Sistine Chapel in Vatican City between 1508 and 1512.

William Shakespeare, a well-known British playwright, wrote many humorous and tragic plays that are still performed today. These include *A Midsummer Night's Dream* and *Macbeth*. Other British writers have created lasting characters, such as Sir Arthur Conan Doyle's Sherlock Holmes.

Europeans today enjoy local radio stations, newspapers, and television networks. Countries produce movies in their native languages. Many European actors and actresses have found fame in Hollywood. England's Hugh Grant has been seen in movies such as *Four Weddings and a Funeral*, *Notting Hill*, and *Bridget Jones' Diary*. Sean Connery, from Scotland, is perhaps best known for his role as James Bond in seven movies.

"Johnson and Son" is one of Salvador Dali's works.

Fast Facts

In Austria, the Salzburg Festival attracts visitors wishing to see productions of well-known operas.

Some consider Vincent van Gogh one of Europe's best painters—even though he was not very successful when he was alive in the 1800s. In 10 years, he produced about 900 paintings and 1,100 drawings.

Of all the recorded music sold around the world, about one-third is made by European musicians.

Dracula is a fictional character, but may have been based on a real person. Prince Vlad Tepes ruled in Romania's Transylvania in the 1400s. He committed many brutal murders.

Europeans have danced ballet since the 1400s. Today, it is an art form enjoyed across Europe and around the world.

Sports

Europeans call soccer football. Football is Europe's most popular sport. It is the national sport of most European countries, and is played on streets and in stadiums from Great Britain to Spain. Professional and semi-professional teams play within their home countries and against other European nations. The best men's and women's teams compete in the World Cup, which takes place every 4 years.

Golf was developed in Scotland. The Honorable Company of Edinburgh Golfers, the world's first golf club, was established in 1744. Amateur golfers enjoy the game across the continent, while professionals compete in tournaments such as the British Open. Tennis is also popular with both amateur and professional athletes. On the professional tour, players compete in European tournaments, such as Wimbledon in Great Britain and the French Open in France.

Football is very popular in Europe. Fans often cheer almost as loudly for teams from other countries as for teams from their own country.

Fast Facts

Ancient Rome's Colosseum, built in AD 79, was a popular place to watch sporting events, including fights between wild animals and professional fighters called gladiators.

Football originated in Europe. It developed in Great Britain in the 1800s.

Many tourists travel to Monaco to watch car races, including the Monaco Grand Prix and the Monte Carlo Rally.

Sweden has a national tradition called *allemansrätten*. It allows people to hike and camp anywhere in the country—even on private lands—as long as they respect nature and other people's privacy.

The Matterhorn is a major mountain in the Swiss Alps. Many people believed it was impossible to climb this mountain because of its steep sides. It was finally **scaled** in 1865. People today come from around the world to try to climb the steep mountain.

Hockey is also a popular sport. Other professional sports include bullfighting in Spain and Portugal, rugby and cricket in Great Britain, and car racing in Monaco.

Amateur athletes can participate in many sporting activities. Many Scandinavians own country cabins and enjoy winter sports such as skiing. Swedes take advantage of the country's many forests and lakes to camp, hike, and fish. Russians also fish, sometimes through holes in the ice on frozen lakes.

Skiing is a major draw in the continent's many mountainous areas. Major ski resorts include St. Moritz and Zermatt in Switzerland, and Innsbruck and Salzburg in Austria. Mountain rivers are used for white-water rafting.

On the Mediterranean Sea, diving is popular, as are windsurfing and sailing. Visitors further east can **spelunk** in Slovakia and Hungary's caves and caverns to see mineral and rock formations called **stalactites** and **stalagmites**.

Cricket is a popular sport in Great Britain. It is also enjoyed around the world in countries such as India, South Africa, and New Zealand.

Brain Teasers

1 What continent is connected to Europe's eastern side?

2 What is the world's smallest country? How many people live there?

3 What is Europe's largest mammal?

4 What fortress is located in Moscow, Russia?

5 What are two makes of automobiles that originated in Europe?

6 Where are Europe's major stock exchanges located?

7 How much of Africa eventually became a British colony? How much of Asia?

8 What is a country called when a king or queen rules it?

9 What are Europe's three major language groups?

10 Who was a well-known British playwright?

For More Information

Books

Check the school or public library for more information about Europe. The following books have useful information about the continent:

Sayre, April Pulley. *Europe*. Connecticut: Twenty-First Century Books, 1998.

Striveildi, Cheryl. *Europe*. Minnesota: Buddy Books, 2003.

Weintraub, Aileen. *Discovering Europe's Land, People, and Wildlife*. New Jersey: Myreportlinks.com, 2004.

Web sites

You can also go online and have a look at the following Web sites:

Lonely Planet: Europe
www.lonelyplanet.com/destinations/loc-eur.htm

Europe for Visitors
http://europeforvisitors.com

Europe Travel and Vacation Information
www.informationeurope.com

Visit Europe
www.visiteurope.com

IPL Kidspace: Culture Quest
www.ipl.org/div/kidspace/cquest/europe/europe.html

Glossary

aurochs long-horned wild oxes

canals man-made waterways used for transportation

Christian a person who believes in Jesus Christ's teachings

colonies communities of people who have settled together

cubism using geometric shapes to create a picture

density very close together with little space between

dialects local forms of a language spoken in a specific region

dictatorship a place that is ruled by one leader who uses power harshly

diversity having a large variety

emigrate to leave one's country of origin to move to another country

endangered when so few of a species remain that they need protection in order to survive

flamenco dancing a type of dance featuring hand clapping and stamping feet

gothic a type of architecture featuring pointed arches and high, curved ceilings

Industrial Revolution a time in the late 1800s when large-scale factory work and production lines were first developed

medieval from the period of time called the Middle Ages

merchant shipping fleets ships that carry merchandise for trade with other countries

nomads people who travel in search of food

nuclear reactors devices that help produce nuclear energy

outcropping a rock that sticks up from the surface of the soil

peat partially decomposed organic debris

persecution to be harmed or harassed

plateaus hills or mountains with level tops

Roman Empire the areas Ancient Rome ruled, stretching from Great Britain to North Africa to the Middle East

scaled climbed up or over

Scandinavia an area comprising Norway, Sweden, Denmark, Finland, Iceland, and the Faroe Islands

slaves people who are forced to work tiring jobs for no pay

spelunk to explore caves

stalactites limestone pillars that hang from a cave's roof

stalagmites limestone pillars that rise from a cave's floor

steppes treeless plains

stock exchanges places where people meet to buy and sell stocks and shares of companies

surrealist art that attempts to illustrate the subconscious, or mental activities beyond one's awareness

trade the activity of buying and selling goods between countries

visual arts artwork, such as painting or sculpture, that can be viewed and appreciated

Index